MUMMIES

BY JIM OLLHOFF

Visit us at

WWW.ABDOPUBLISHING.COM

Published by ABDO Publishing Company, 4940 Viking Drive, Suite 622, Edina, Minnesota 55435.
Copyright ©2007 by Abdo Consulting Group, Inc. International copyrights reserved in all countries.
No part of this book may be reproduced in any form without written permission from the publisher.
ABDO & Daughters™ is a trademark and logo of ABDO Publishing Company.

Printed in the United States.

Editors: John Hamilton/Tad Bornhoft
Graphic Design: Sue Hamilton
Cover Design: Neil Klinepier
Cover Illustration: Mummies, WireImage
Interior Photos and Illustrations: p 1 Wax figure of Boris Karloff, AP/Wideworld; p 3 Illustration, Zedcor;
p 4 Valley of the Kings, Mary Evans Picture Library; p 5 Howard Carter sees Tut's sarcophagus, Mary
Evans Picture Library; p 6 Carter and Carnarvon, Mary Evans Picture Library; p 7 Removal of treasures,
Mary Evans Picture Library; p 8 Howard Carter, courtesy the University of Bonn; p 9 Howard Carter and
Lord Carnarvon, courtesy the University of Bonn; p 10 Carter in Tut's tomb, Mary Evans Picture Library;
p 11 Tut's treasure, Mary Evans Picture Library; p 12 Anubis, Photo Researchers, Inc.; p 13 Mummies
dicing, Mary Evans Picture Library; p 14 Mummified monkey, AP/Wideworld; p 15 Mummification
process, Photo Researchers, Inc.; pp 16-17 Treasures for the mummy, Photo Researchers, Inc.; p 18 Incan
mummy, AP/Wideworld; p 19 Peruvian mummy, AP/Wideworld; pp 20-21 Tollund Man, Corbis;
p 22 Tut's golden mask, Corbis; p 23 *The Mummy* (1932) movie poster, courtesy Universal Pictures;
p 24 *The Mummy's Hand* photograph, courtesy Universal Pictures; *The Mummy's Tomb* photograph,
courtesy Universal Pictures; *The Mummy* (1959) photograph, courtesy Hammer Film Productions,
The Mummy's Shroud photograph, courtesy Hammer Film Productions; p 25 Lon Chaney, Jr., in *The
Mummy's Ghost,* courtesy Universal Pictures; p 26 *Blood from the Mummy's Tomb* movie poster, courtesy
Hammer Film Productions/EMI Films; *The Mummy* (1999) photograph, courtesy Universal Pictures; *The
Mummy Returns* movie card, courtesy Universal Pictures; p 27 *The Mummy Returns* movie poster, courtesy
Universal Pictures; p 28 Visitor at Tut exhibit, AP/Wideworld; p 29 Viscera coffin, AP/Wideworld;
p 30 Professionals examine Tut's mummy, AP/Wideworld; p 31 Statue of Tut's head, AP/Wideworld

Library of Congress Cataloging-in-Publication Data

Ollhoff, Jim, 1959-
   Mummies / Jim Ollhoff.
      p. cm. -- (The world of horror)
   Includes bibliographical references and index.
   ISBN-13: 978-1-59928-772-0 (alk. paper)
   ISBN-10: 1-59928-772-2 (alk. paper)
   1. Mummies. I. Title.

GN293.O55 2007
393'.3--dc22
                            2006032731

CONTENTS

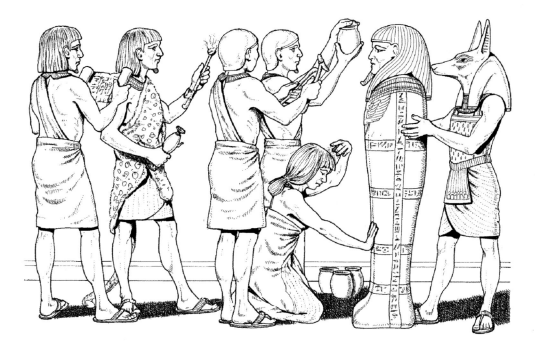

DEATH COMES ON SWIFT WINGS

A gold-covered wall rose in front of the explorers. It was November 1922. After years of searching, archaeologist Howard Carter had finally found the ancient tomb of Egyptian King Tutankhamun, and it looked as though tomb raiders may not have raided it beforehand.

Archaeologists had found many Egyptian tombs before, but all had been robbed and ransacked centuries earlier. Now, for the first time ever, Carter stood before an undisturbed tomb. He knew that in front of him was one of the greatest discoveries in history.

Carter saw the unbroken original seal of King Tutankhamun on the door, so he knew that the grave had not been robbed. Egyptian priests had placed the seal across the ancient door when King Tutankhamun was buried—and the seal was still intact. This meant that no human being had set foot in the tomb for over 3,300 years. Carter reached for the door to break open the seal, but one of his Egyptian partners stopped him, pointing to hieroglyphics above the door. Carter read the inscription: "Death comes on swift wings to he who disturbs the peace of the King."

Below: Entrance to the Valley of the Kings, near Luxor, Egypt.

4

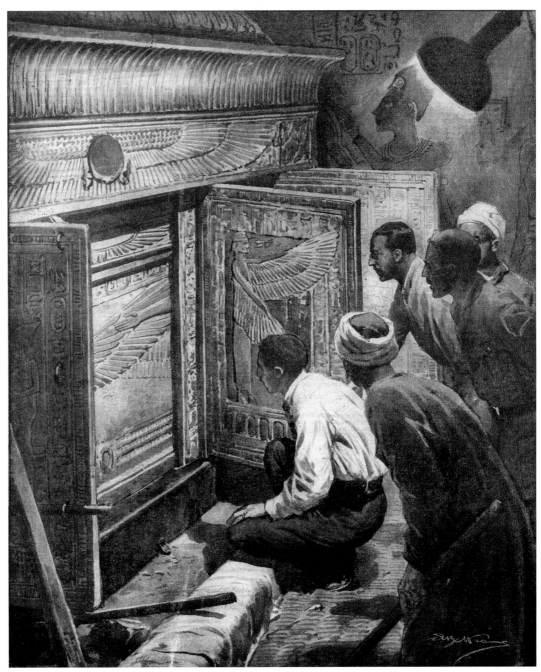

Above: In November 1922, Howard Carter discovered the tomb of Egyptian King Tutankhamun. He was awed by the wondrous treasures he found inside. In February 1923, he beheld the intact sarcophagus, or coffin, of the Egyptian pharaoh. Inside lay the mummifed body of the boy king who died in 1323 B.C.

Ignoring the curse as a silly superstition, Carter opened the tomb and went inside. But outside the tomb, a cobra suddenly swallowed Carter's pet canary. The electricity in the Egyptian city of Cairo went dead at the exact time the tomb was disturbed. Carter's dog, at home thousands of miles away, let out a howl and died. Within a few days, the man who funded the expedition died unexpectedly. Months later, everyone who entered the tomb died strange and mysterious deaths. Death indeed came on swift wings. The curse of the mummy lived on.

At least, that's one version of the story. In other accounts, it's someone else's dog that howls, and the man who funded the expedition dies weeks, not days, later. Other stories say the lights of Cairo went out immediately after the man's death, not when the tomb was entered.

There are many mysterious versions of the curse of Tutankhamun. But it didn't really happen that way. Howard Carter did discover the tomb in 1922, but there were no mysterious deaths. However, people started inventing stories, and then rumors started. Some newspapers even reported these rumors as if they were facts. Many people believed in the mummy's curse. To this day, some still accept the story as truth.

But the truth is that there was no curse. There was no inscription above the door. A cobra did not eat Carter's canary. The lights in Cairo stayed on. Carter's dog didn't die. Members of the expedition lived to a ripe old age. The only untimely death was the Englishman who funded the expedition. Lord Carnarvon died in April 1923, a few months after Carter found the tomb. Carnarvon died of an infection from a cut, which was a common cause of death in the days before antibiotics.

Below: Howard Carter, Lord Carnarvon, and Egyptian archaeologists in King Tut's tomb.

Above: Howard Carter and Lord Carnarvon supervise removal of treasures from King Tutankhamun's tomb.

Many people find the idea of 3,000-year-old curses exciting and mysterious. We're thrilled at the thought of mummies coming to life, punishing those who desecrate their tombs. Books and movies about mummies are very popular. But the modern interest in mummies got its start from one thrilling, true-life adventure: the discovery of the tomb of King Tutankhamun.

THE DISCOVERY OF KING TUT

Below: Howard Carter, the man who discovered King Tut's tomb.

Beginning in 1903, an American businessman named Theodore Davis began paying for a series of explorations in Egypt. These were excavations in which archaeologists dug down to buildings that were long ago covered with sand. Davis and his team worked in the Valley of the Kings, near the modern-day city of Luxor, Egypt. This was a burial site for many of the kings, called pharaohs, of ancient Egypt. One of the archaeologists on Davis' team was Howard Carter. An experienced Egyptologist, Carter had already located the tombs of several kings.

In ancient Egypt, kings were buried with many luxuries, including furniture, food, drink, and chariots—anything that might help them in the afterlife. Kings were also buried with gold, jewels, and lots of expensive things. After a king's burial, grave robbers eventually broke into most tombs and stole everything of value. This is a problem for modern-day archaeologists and historians. Without the artifacts, it is hard to learn about the ancient Egyptian way of life.

Davis wanted to find the tomb of King Tutankhamun (a name often shortened to "King Tut"). Tutankhamun was a boy who rose to the throne at age nine. He ruled Egypt more than 3,300 years ago. He was just a teenager when he died.

Davis' team of archaeologists found several clues that led them to believe Tutankhamun's tomb was nearby. But they could never seem to pinpoint its location. Theodore Davis became convinced there was nothing left to find, so he stopped paying for the expedition.

Howard Carter found a new financial backer, an Englishman named Lord Carnarvon. Carter began digging in the Valley of the Kings again in 1917. He searched for the tomb of Tutankhamun for five more years, with no luck. Carnarvon wanted to give up, but Carter convinced him to look for one more season.

Above: Howard Carter, left, with his financial backer, Lord Carnarvon. After discovering King Tut's tomb, Carter immediately sent word to Carnarvon in England. With extreme patience, Carter waited two weeks for the English lord to join him in Egypt before proceeding to open the tomb.

Above: Howard Carter and staff working at the tomb of King Tutankhamun in 1923.

Above: A small part of the treasure that Howard Carter found in King Tut's tomb.

In November 1921, they gave Tutankhamun one more chance. They removed some ancient buildings that were used as sleeping quarters for the builders of one of the other tombs. When they removed the buildings, they saw a set of stairs that went down.

After removing some of the rocks and debris that had piled up over the centuries, they found a door at the bottom of the stairs. The door was stamped with the seal of King Tutankhamun. Finally, after years of trying, they found the tomb of the king.

Several weeks of careful excavation followed. The team found another door behind the first door. Slowly, they excavated and explored, cataloging everything. Finally, in February 1922, they entered the chamber of King Tutankhamun. They saw a wonderful array of artifacts, which hadn't been seen for more than 3,300 years. They found furniture, statues, chests, and pottery, all inlaid with gold and precious jewels. The mummy of the king himself was decorated with 150 pieces of jewelry.

King Tutankhamun was not an important king in Egypt, and he didn't reign for very long. But he instantly became famous because his tomb was full of all the original burial objects. Tutankhamun quickly became a household name.

WHY DID THEY MAKE MUMMIES?

Above: A depiction of Egyptian afterlife events.

The ancient Egyptians believed in the afterlife. They believed that once you died, your spirit left your body for a while, but then it came back to the body. Reunited, the body and spirit would make the journey through the underworld. The underworld was a dangerous place, full of monsters and wild animals. The deceased needed help from magical spells to get through it safely.

Then, in the underworld, after traveling a long ways, the dead person finally made it to the Hall of Two Truths. Anubis, the jackal-headed god of the underworld, guarded the hall. Anubis had a big scale in front of him. He put the dead person's heart on one side of the scale. On the other side, Anubis placed a

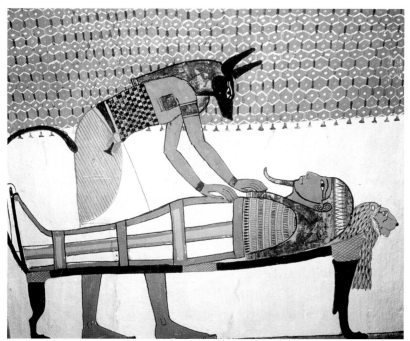

Right: Anubis, the jackal-headed god of the underworld, stands over a sarcophagus.

Above: Prince Setna, son of Ramses II, and Ptahneferka, son of Mernebptah, rise from their sarcophagi and play a game of dice.

feather of Maat, the goddess of truth. If the scale said there were enough good deeds in the person's life, they could move on to the Field of Offerings. This was a wonderful place where there was always enough food to eat. If, however, there were too many bad deeds, then Ammut, the crocodile god, would eat the dead person immediately.

Since the ancient Egyptians believed they needed their bodies again in the afterlife, they spent a lot of time making sure the corpses were as lifelike as possible. The body had to look the same as when a person was alive, or else the spirit wouldn't recognize it. If the dead body decomposed at all, then the spirit couldn't re-enter the body and journey through the underworld.

Mummification, for most of history, was done only for kings or important people. The process was very expensive, and only the very rich could afford it. As time went on, more and more people paid to have it done. Everyone wanted to have a chance in the afterlife.

How Mummies Got Mummified

The Egyptians mummified bodies in a long, careful process. The entire procedure of preparing and wrapping a body took about 70 days. First, the priests and embalmers took the body to a building called the Place of Purification. There, they washed the body with wine and rinsed it with water. They also packed the body in a powder called *natron,* which is similar to a combination of salt and baking soda. Natron pulled the moisture out of the body. Mummies had to be very dry, so that bacteria couldn't live inside the corpse. Otherwise, it would start to decompose. Natron kept the mummies dry.

Next, the body was moved to a place called the House of Beauty. Here, the embalmers made a small cut in the body's side, and removed several of the internal organs. The lungs, stomach, liver, and intestines were removed. Then, the embalmers drove a hook up through the nostrils and pulled out the brain. The ancient Egyptians didn't really understand what the brain did, so they threw it away. However, they left the heart intact in the body because they believed it was the center of thoughts and feelings. You couldn't get through the afterlife without it.

Below: A pharaoh's mummified pet monkey.

After removing the internal organs, the embalmers packed the body with natron to dry it out. Then they wrapped the internal organs with linen and packed them in natron also. The embalmers put the mummified organs in containers called canopic jars. These were ceramic jars decorated with the head of an Egyptian god on the top. The jar with the god Imsety protected the liver. The lungs went into a jar with Hapy, a baboon-headed god. Duamutef, a jackal-headed god, looked after the person's stomach. The falcon-headed god, Qebehsenuef, protected the intestines.

The body was allowed to sit for over a month in order to let the natron dry it out. After about 40 days, the body was washed with water, and then covered with oil to keep the skin elastic.

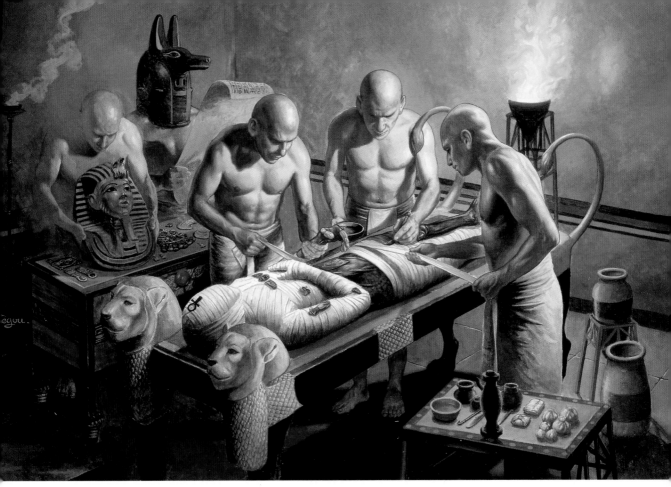

The embalmers removed the natron and put the organs, still wrapped in linen, back into the body. Then they stuffed the body with sawdust, linen, or bags of natron so that it would look as lifelike as possible. The embalmers then inserted artificial eyes, which were usually painted stones.

The next step was to wrap the mummy with linen strips. Wrapping the mummy could take up to two weeks. The process began with embalmers applying scented oil to the body. Next the head and fingers were wrapped with linen. Then the rest of the body was wrapped. Magic amulets were placed between the linens. The dead person needed the magic amulets for protection in the dangerous journey through the underworld.

The body was now completely wrapped up with linen strips. The priests then applied a sticky sap to the linens so that the strips would hold together. During this process, priests read magic spells to give the dead person protection and support in the underworld. When the wrapping was finished, the priests wrote a few magic spells on a scroll, and then put it into the hands of the mummy.

Above: An illustration of King Tut undergoing the exacting mummification process.

Below: Items needed in the ancient Egyptian afterlife.

The priests believed people might forget the magic spells as they made their way through the underworld, so having some notes helped them on their journey.

Next, a final, large cloth was wrapped around the mummy. The priests painted the cloth with a likeness of Osiris, the Egyptian god of the dead. They lowered the body into a coffin, and then the coffin was put inside a larger coffin. The larger coffin was painted with a portrait mask—a likeness of the person inside. This was done so the spirit would recognize the body.

The priests performed one final magic ritual, called "opening the mouth." They touched the mummy with various implements and recited magic incantations. They made an offering, often with a bull's heart, and anointed the mummy. The ritual was performed so that the spirit could get back into its body.

Lastly, the mummy was placed in a tomb with food, drinks, clothing, furniture—all the things they might need on the trip through the afterlife. Sometimes servants volunteered to go along. They were ritually killed, and their bodies placed in the tomb along with their masters. Many tombs even had mummified dogs and cats in them to keep the deceased company in the afterlife.

MUMMIES AROUND THE WORLD

While mummies from Egypt are the most famous, the Egyptians were not the first to mummify their dead. In South America, in what is now Chile, there was a tribe known as the Chinchoros. They were making mummies 2,000 years before the Egyptians.

To prepare their dead, the Chinchoros removed the internal organs and preserved them. They put wood and other materials in the bodies to keep them from shrinking. Then they covered the bodies with clay and painted designs on them.

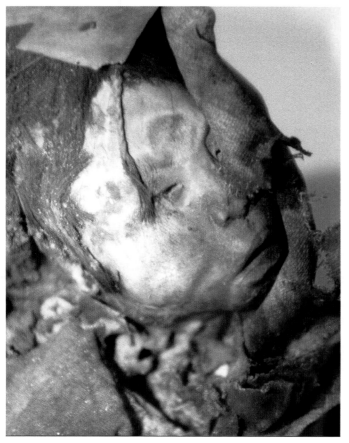

Further north, the Inca civilization (1100 to 1500 A.D.) also mummified their dead. They arranged each body in a fetal position, wrapped it in leather, and then often placed the mummy in a large basket or jar.

Many of the Incan mummies were sacrifices made to appease the mountain gods. The bodies were mummified high in the mountains. The cold, dry air preserved the mummies for hundreds of years.

Left: The face of a 500-year-old Incan mummy.

Above: A 700-year-old mummy found in Arequipa, Peru, a city just south of Lima. The man is believed to have died while in his mid-30s.

Sometimes, the preservation of dead bodies is accidental. One of the most famous cases is called Tollund Man, who died about 350 B.C. The body was found in Denmark in 1950. It was so well preserved that the discoverers thought it was a recent murder, so they called the police.

Tollund Man was found in a peat bog. A peat bog is a particular kind of wetland. Lots of dead plant material, called peat, builds up in the water. This makes the water mildly acidic, which kills bacteria. Also, oxygen is used up in bogs, which slows decomposition. Bodies buried in bogs stay very well preserved. Tollund Man was so well preserved that scientists were able to determine exactly what he ate for his last meal. In fact, they knew he didn't shave the day he died because they could see the whisker stubble on his chin.

Right: The Tollund Man.

MUMMY MOVIE MANIA

Across the world, people were riveted by news reports about the treasures of King Tutankhamun. Some people, and even some newspapers, reported stories about "the curse of the mummy." Of course, Hollywood saw this as a perfect subject for some scary movies.

Right: The priceless golden mask of King Tutankhamun. On the night of September 10, 1996, a robber hid inside the Egyptian Museum in Cairo, Egypt. He pried open a case of King Tut's treasures and stuffed gold jewelry in his pockets and socks. Guards caught him the very next day.

The Mummy (1932)

The Mummy wasn't the first mummy movie ever made, but it was the best one made up to that time. The famous Boris Karloff stars as Imhotep. He is brought back to life, and then takes the form of a creepy old man who tries to bring back his long-lost love, Ankh-es-en-Amon. Her spirit resides in the girlfriend of an archaeologist. Imhotep terrorizes anyone who stands in his way. The story in this movie involves the concept of reincarnation. Reincarnation is the belief that when people die, only their physical bodies die. The spirits of people never die, but are simply born into new bodies. Contrary to what the movie says, the ancient Egyptians did not believe in reincarnation.

Above: A movie poster for Universal Pictures' *The Mummy.* Starring Boris Karloff, the film was a huge box-office success.

The Mummy's Hand (1940)

In ancient Egypt, Princess Ananka dies, and is buried. However, the high priest Kharis is so in love with her that he refuses to believe she is gone forever. He tries to bring her back from the dead by reading magic spells from a forbidden book. Before he can succeed, the king's guards find him. For his crime, Kharis is sentenced to be mummified alive. A group called the Priests of Karnack commit themselves to making sure no one ever finds the tombs of Kharis or Princess Ananka. Thousands of years pass. In modern-day Egypt, an American archaeologist finds the tomb of Kharis. However, the Priests of Karnack are still protecting the tombs. The priests bring back Kharis the mummy to stop those who are seeking the tomb of Princess Ananka.

The Mummy's Tomb (1942)

In a sequel set 30 years after *The Mummy's Hand*, we learn that Kharis the mummy was not killed in the last movie. He comes to the United States to hunt down all the members of the expedition that opened the tomb of Princess Ananka. The Priests of Karnack are the real villains here. The mummy is forced to do the bidding of the high priest. In this movie, we almost feel sorry for the mummy.

The Mummy (1959)

This movie, which starred Peter Cushing and Christopher Lee, took its inspiration and characters from *The Mummy's Hand*. In this story, archaeologists discover the tomb of Princess Ananka. Kharis, imprisoned as a mummy for his love for the princess, is brought to life. As her eternal guard, he wreaks vengeance on all those who desecrate her tomb.

The Mummy's Shroud (1967)

In ancient Egypt, there is a battle in the royal palace. The king is killed, and a loyal slave whisks the young king's son, Kah-To-Bey, out of the palace. However, as they try to escape, both the slave and the boy die in the desert heat. Thousands of years later, a modern-day archaeological team discovers the tomb of the slave and Kah-To-Bey. The slave, brought back to life as a mummy, takes revenge on the archaeologists for disturbing the boy's tomb.

Above: Lon Chaney, Jr., stars as the mummy Kharis in 1944's *The Mummy's Ghost*. This was the third film in a series of Universal Pictures mummy movies. Preceeding it was 1940's *The Mummy's Hand* and 1942's *The Mummy's Tomb*.

Blood from the Mummy's Tomb (1971)

Officials in ancient Egypt execute an evil queen for practicing black magic. The officials seal her in a secret tomb. When a modern-day archaeologist discovers her tomb, she awakens. The evil queen starts to take over the body of the archaeologist's daughter so that she can collect magic artifacts, which will complete her resurrection. This movie was one of the first to show a mummy that wasn't wrapped up in linens.

The Mummy (1999)

This popular movie stars Brendan Fraser, Rachel Weisz, and Arnold Vosloo. The heroes stumble upon the tomb of Imhotep, mummified and buried for thousands of years. They accidentally bring the mummy to life. Imhotep seeks to bring Anck-Su-Namun, his long-lost love, back from the dead. The heroes must stop Imhotep before he becomes too powerful. In this movie, the mummy is fast, instead of the slow, lumbering mummies of the older movies.

The Mummy Returns (2001)

A sequel to the 1999 film, *The Mummy Returns* features the reincarnated spirit of Anck-Su-Namun working to raise Imhotep. She succeeds, and then the two try to find the Bracelet of Anubis. This magical bracelet gives Imhotep the power to control vast ghostly armies. With these armies, Imhotep plans to rule the world. The 10-year-old son of our heroes accidentally gets the bracelet stuck on his arm, so the villains kidnap the child. Our heroes have to save their son and stop Imhotep from raising his ghostly armies.

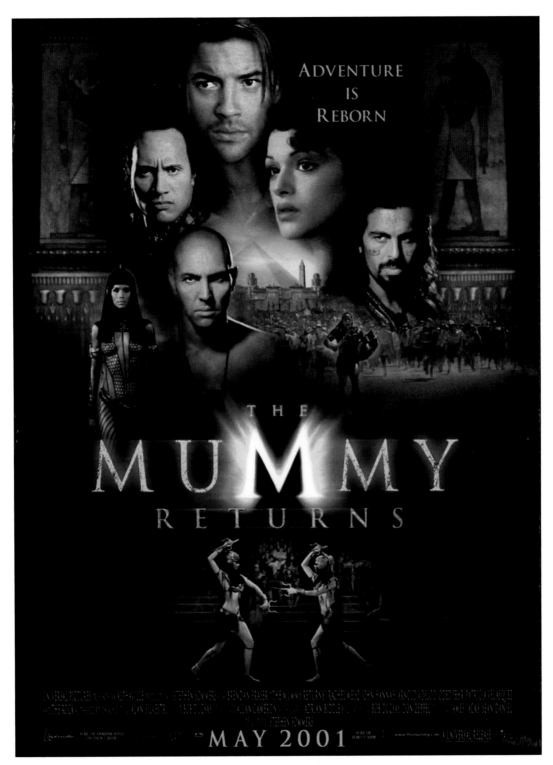

Above: A movie poster for *The Mummy Returns.* This popular movie sequel brought back the mummy-hunting characters of Evelyn (Rachel Weisz) and Rick O'Connell (Brendan Fraser).

WHY DO WE LOVE OUR MUMMIES?

The Egyptians took great care in preparing their dead. It was a highly religious process, with lots of magic thrown in. They had a passionate belief in the afterlife. Their rituals were secretive, their belief in the afterlife was strong, and they claimed to understand the mysteries of life and death. Everything they did was directed toward raising someone from the dead, so it's fun to believe that they actually knew how to do that.

Above: A visitor enters the "Tutankhamun and the Golden Age of Pharaohs" exhibition at the Los Angeles County Museum of Art on June 15, 2005. Its massive popularity made it difficult for everyone to see the exhibit.

If you combine secret rituals, magic spells, curses that last forever, and love that never dies, you have the perfect mummy story. Most of the stories told today are about a guardian or lover of a princess, who comes back from the dead 3,000 years later to continue life. We like the idea of that kind of devotion. We like the idea of love that never dies, that stretches across the sands of time. In some way or another, those kinds of stories will always be with us.

Left: One of four mini-coffins that held the mummified internal organs of King Tutankhamun. It is a miniature replica of Tut's golden funeral sarcophagus.

GLOSSARY

ARCHAEOLOGIST

A scientist who studies physical objects to learn about historic people, their activities, and practices. Archaeologists will seek out and excavate fossil relics, artifacts, monuments, and other remains of a culture to learn more about the people who made them.

DESECRATE

To treat disrespectfully or violate the character of something considered sacred or hallowed.

Above: Professionals examine the 3,300-year-old mummy of King Tutankhamun in January 2005. Modern technology has shown that he probably died of natural causes, but may have suffered a badly broken leg shortly before his death.

EGYPTOLOGIST
A person who studies ancient Egypt, its people, artifacts, and culture. A highly developed ancient Egyptian society existed for thousands of years, providing much to be discovered and explored.

EXPEDITION
A journey made for a specific purpose, such as exploration of a region or scientific discovery.

HIEROGLYPHS
Characters in the writing system used by ancient Egyptians. Hieroglyphs are mostly of a pictorial nature. The study of ancient Egypt was greatly advanced when hieroglyphs were deciphered, or translated.

LINEN
Strong, shiny cloth made from the fiber of flax plants.

PHARAOH
The title given to the ruler, or king, of ancient Egypt. The pharaoh was believed to be the child of the sun god Ra.

TOMB
A house, chamber, or vault built for the dead. Some tombs, such as those built for pharaohs, are permanently sealed.

Right: An ancient statue of King Tutankhamun showing what he looked like on the day he died.

INDEX

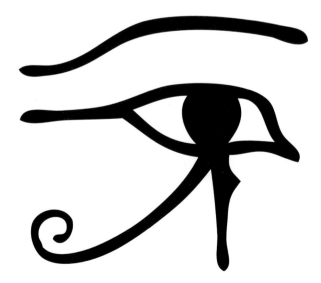